THESE ARE OUR BODIES

FOR MIDDLE SCHOOL

PARENT BOOK

Church Publishing Incorporated
19 East 34th Street, New York, NY 10016
www.churchpublishing.org

Cover design by Jennifer Kopec, 2 Pug Design
Typeset by Progressive Publishing Services

ISBN-13: 978-1-60674-315-7 (pbk.)
ISBN-13: 978-1-60674-316-4 (ebook)

Printed in the United States of America

CONTENTS

INTRODUCTION

God created humanity in God's own image, in the divine image God created them.

—Genesis 1:27, *NRSV*

The only way I know how to teach anyone to love God, and how I myself can love God, is to love what God loves, which is everything and everyone, including you and including me![1]

—Richard Rohr

We love because [God] first loved us. If we love each other, God remains in us and [God's] love is made perfect in us.

—1 John 4:19, 12, CEB

As a people made in the image of God, our bodies and sexuality are sacred gifts that we seek to understand and use as faithful people; affirming that we, and our sexuality as part

1 Rohr, Richard. *Franciscan Mysticism: I AM That Which I Am Seeking* (Center for Action and Contemplation: 2012), disc 2; accessed https://cac.org/love-god-in-what-is-right-in-front-of-you-2016-01-17/ January 23, 2016.

of creation, are good. As Christians seeking to live a life worthy of our calling, we are called to explore our sexuality in the context of our faith. One of the greatest joys and responsibilities as parents[2] is to teach children that they are loved by God, body and all.

Your middle-schooler has begun the *These Are Our Bodies* program. This *Parent Guide* is *your* first step on the journey. We know that most effective teaching about sexuality includes both children and parents. You know that your children have been watching you and learning from you since birth. Your most basic gestures, attitudes, and comments teach your children how to think about their bodies. Now that your child is in middle school, the information that they need to be informed and empowered is changing. One goal of this program is to help you communicate knowledge, skills, and values to your middle-schoolers and to make that vital connection between faith and sexuality. Parents sometimes feel anxious about tackling the next stage of questions, and we want to give parents the information you need to jump right into conversations with your growing child.

Although you are not the only source of information for your child, you are the primary educator—you are the most

2 We recognize that all families look different; we use "parent" in the broadest sense throughout this program. Parent refers to all those primary caretakers who have children or youth in their custody—single parents, single moms, single dads, grandparents, aunts, uncles, foster parents, adoptive parents, divorced or widowed parents, and anyone else who has responsibility for raising children.

consistent, the most present, and the most responsive. You are the one who can give them a foundation of values, attitudes, and skills that will guide them into their young adult years. The realization that you are the primary sexuality educator of your child can be the beginning of an exciting journey, and the entryway to a host of parental anxieties and questions. Many parents feel unprepared for this part of their parenting. Your child needs to hear your voice—your voice on sex, your voice on behavior, your voice on attitudes, and your voice on how faith connects to sexuality. How do you make that happen?

We hear parents ask for guidance in crafting messages to their children. Messages that:

- combat the often selfish and cynical messages about love, bodies, and sex that we hear from our society
- tell the truth and challenge the incomplete and stunted teachings our children receive from our modern culture
- connect faith and sexuality
- ask, "Where is God in this?"

Participating in *These Are Our Bodies* paves the way for more open communication between middle-schoolers and parents, including the connection between sexuality and faith.

These Are Our Bodies is a developmentally appropriate, creatively interactive, faith-based approach to sexuality that places human sexuality in the context of faith. Concepts such as God's creation, scripture, and sexuality as a gift from God are woven throughout the sessions. The conversations and teaching around the stewardship of gifts, responsible behavior, and God's grace and love form the foundation of the theology of the program.

The sessions in *These Are Our Bodies* program materials (age-based *Leader Guide, Parent Book,* and *Participant Book*) are each designed to teach concepts around our faith in ways that connect with young people and give them opportunities to strengthen their faith. The program includes content that makes a connection between our faith and sexuality. Participants will gain assurance that their growing and developing is normal and expected. As they continue their journey toward adulthood and independence, the program will provide opportunities to bridge the gap between their everyday lives and their faith lives by creating a holy space for them to ask their questions and receive honest answers.

The *These Are Our Bodies Foundation Book* is the companion volume to the *These Are Our Bodies* program, including the middle-school level. Parents are encouraged to get and read this *Foundation Book* as well. Grounded in the Episcopal faith tradition, it provides theological background and practical guidance about the complexities of sexuality in today's world. You will find this book a helpful addition to the middle-school program, and relevant for other ages as well.

The *Foundation Book* includes essays about the role of sexuality and practical guides to inform church educators, parents, leaders, or anyone who seeks to broaden their knowledge on this subject. Organized into four sections: The Theological, The Ethical, The Biological, and The Practical, each explores the complexity of sexuality and is written both to be read on its own and as part of the unified book. The extensive annotated resource section and glossary round out the book to give readers the information they need for further exploration on topics of sexuality.

Section III, The Biological, expands on the role of parenting in healthy development and provides a review of developmental theories, moral development psychology, and faith development across the lifespan. The research and theories of leading psychologists underpin our understanding of the needs of children, including the healthy growth of their bodies and their moral development. We conclude this section with a discussion of faith development and its implications in understanding the complexity of human sexuality.

Section IV, The Practical, gives adults the tools needed to understand the stages of child development that inform our life and ministry with children and teens. This section also gives parents the background knowledge and information they need to be the primary sexuality educators for their children. The review of development (physical, emotional and social, spiritual and moral) will benefit anyone working with or raising children and teens.

This *Parent Book,* as part of the middle-school program, consists of 10 sessions that teach the facts that middle-schoolers need to know, make the connection between sexuality and faith, and put you, the parent, right in the middle.

Participants have their *Participant Book,* which will be theirs to use during the program and to keep as a reference after the program is over. This *Parent Book,* however, is meant to be a resource just for you. This book will keep you informed about each session. In each chapter, you will read about what your middle-schooler is learning. You will be invited to reflect on some of the scripture that they are studying. Each chapter also includes journal questions that will help you connect faith with sexuality and with parenting. You'll learn new ways to think about sexuality and how faith is relevant to understanding the complexities of sexuality. In this program both participants and parents learn and grow together.

Our hope is that you will talk about learning in conjunction with your middle-schooler. This program and this book work in harmony to open the lines of communication between you and your middle-schooler. As we walk in faith, we benefit the most from a shared journey.

PREVIEW SESSION

A Prayer for Young Persons:

God our Father, you see your children growing up in an unsteady and confusing world: Show them that your ways give more life than the ways of the world, and that following you is better than chasing after selfish goals. Help them to take failure, not as a measure of their worth, but as a chance for a new start. Give them strength to hold their faith in you, and to keep alive their joy in your creation; through Jesus Christ our Lord.[3] *Amen.*

One of the main goals of *These Are Our Bodies* is to help users form a group that provides a safe place for participants to

3 Book of Common Prayer, 829.

honestly and openly engage the content of the program. In the church—when we do our most important work—we often form what are called *covenant groups*. Covenant groups form to help their members grapple with difficult topics and grow together.[4]

The biblical concept of *covenant* flows from motifs in the Old Testament. In Genesis, we learn that God formed a covenant with Noah and set the rainbow in the sky as a reminder of that covenant. In Genesis, we also hear the call for the people to be *God's* people in a deep covenant relationship. In the Book of Common Prayer, the theme of covenant weaves through the Celebration and Blessing of a Marriage. Today, we see covenants as promises between people.

As we embrace the concept of covenant in *These Are Our Bodies,* both participants and leaders make promises to each other in our HOPE ground rules, which we review at the start of every session:

H—Honesty
O—Openness
P—Privacy
E—Enthusiasm

4 This theme of *covenant* not only infuses our group ground rules for the program, it encompasses an overarching ethic of love, grace, and compassion as the foundation of the teaching and in our lives as faithful people. As the program progresses, explore this theme to retell the story of God's grace in our lives and how that unearned love compels us to love others. In the words of Standing Commission on Liturgy and Music, "God's covenant of creating, redeeming, and sustaining love, shape our lives as Christians in relation to God and to God's creation; this calls us to live with love and compassion, justice and peace toward all creatures, friend or foe, neighbor or stranger." (*Liturgical Resources 1: I Will Bless You and You Will Be a Blessing* (New York: Church Publishing, 2015), Supplemental Materials: Appendices of the Report of the Standing Commission on Liturgy and Music, 28.

- As we begin the program, what are your hopes for your middle-schooler in this program?

- What would *you* like to gain from this program?

Parents Are Key

- As you read Chapter 21: Parents Are the Key (page 177) in the *These Are Our Bodies Foundation Book*, write down some of your key insights and takeaways here:

Listening shows love and acceptance.

The first task of love is to listen.[5]
—Paul Tillich

The central mantra of the Jewish people is "Hear, O Israel."
Listen. The command implies that one can hear
that the revelation is still happening.[6]
— Michael Lerner

Listening is an integral part of relationships. Listening is essential to our understanding others and is a gift that we can give to people in our lives. Suppressing our own need to give advice or to ask questions will allow your middle-schooler the space and grace they need to solve their own problems and discover the person they are striving to become.

PACK: Hints for Listening

***P**ay Attention:* Turn to face your child, open up your body and avoid crossing your arms.

5 Tillich, Paul. *Love, Power, and Justice: Ontological Analyses and Ethical Applications* (Oxford University Press, Oxford, 1960), 84.

6 Lerner, Michael. *Jewish Renewal: Path to Healing and Transformation, A* (New York: HarperCollins, 1994), 78.

Simone Weil wrote, "Attention is the rarest and purest form of generosity."[7]

***A**ffirm:* Give affirming nonverbals like head nodding and eye contact.

***C**larify*: Repeat back what you are hearing using facts and the feelings your middle-schooler may be experiencing. At this age, especially, they need help identifying their feelings. When they are trying to communicate, they often use words like *angry, mad, sad,* or *happy* to describe their emotions. You can help by identifying their underlying feelings by giving them words like, *frustration, betrayal,* or *joy*. You could say, "It sounds like you feel____________ when ____________ happens." Because this statement is a best guess at what they are thinking and feeling, allow your child to correct or revise your estimate. In this process, kids learn to value both their emotions and the details of an event.

***K**eep*: Keep the conversation going by using open-ended statements like:

- I am interested in hearing what happened.
- I am here. I am listening. I have the time.
- Tell me more about that.

7 Foer, Jonathan Safran. "How Not to Be Alone." *The New York Times*, June 8, 2013.

Use *statements*, which keep the emphasis on the person talking, instead of *questions*, which shift the focus back to you.

- Use this space to record your thoughts and feelings about PACK:

A Parent's Prayer

Teach me to listen, O God, to those nearest me, my family, my friends, my co-workers.

Help me to be aware that no matter what words I hear, the message is, "Accept the person I am. Listen to me."

Teach me to listen, my caring God, to those far from me—the whisper of the hopeless, the plea of the forgotten, the cry of the anguished.

Teach me to listen, O God my Mother, to myself. Help me to be less afraid to trust the voice inside in the deepest part of me.

Teach me to listen, Holy Spirit, for your voice—in busyness and in boredom, in certainty and doubt, in noise and in silence.

Teach me, Lord, to listen.[8] *Amen.*

8 Harter, Michael. *Hearts on Fire: Praying with Jesuits* (St. Louis: Institute of Jesuit Sources, 1993), 30.

SESSION 1

YOU ARE GOD'S CREATION

A Prayer to God, the Spirit:[9]

O God,
You are Spirit;
You are wind;
You are breath.
You meet us in the wonders of creation,
in the awe of wonderful things,
in the terror of fearful things.
You blow among the fallen leaves,
the broken branches,

9 Emeritus Professor William Loader FAHA, Murdoch University, Western Australia. Used with Permission.

the whining pain
and the whirlwinds of delight.
Your wind gently touches our brow
with comfort and caress;
your forgiveness raises us to life;
your challenge disturbs our tidy piles
and spreads opportunities before our eyes.
Gentle Spirit, breathe on us your life.
Strong Spirit, open our closed doors to your compassion;
Universal Spirit, inspire us to sing and sigh for justice;
Spirit of Jesus, teach us to walk,
to work, to pray, to live, to love,
your way.
Awaken our dreams,
expand our visions,
heal us for hope,
through Jesus Christ our Lord. Amen.

You Are God's Creation

In this session, participants explored God's declaration of "very good" in the story of creation and looked at scripture passages related to the human body. They also began to claim the adjectives "beautiful" and "wonderful" for themselves, recognizing that they are made in the image of God.

In the creation story, humanity is created last. The *Common English Bible* translation is an especially beautiful account of these two important verses:

> Then God said, "Let us make humanity in our image to resemble us so that they may take charge of the fish of the sea, the birds in the sky, the livestock, all the earth, and all the crawling things on earth." God created humanity in God's own image, in the divine image God created them, male and female God created them.
>
> —Genesis 1:26–27, *CEB*

In the *NRSV*, we see the metaphor of likeness:

> Then God said, "Let us make humankind in our image, according to our likeness; and let them have dominion over the fish of the sea, and over the birds of the air, and over the cattle, and over all the wild animals of the earth, and over every creeping thing that creeps upon the earth." So God created humankind in his image, in the image of God he created them; male and female he created them . . .
>
> —Genesis 1:26–27, *NRSV*

As parents, we are entrusted with the care of our children, yet each child is first a child of God. Reflect on the following questions, recording your answers in the space provided:

- How do these passages help you to see your child through God's perspective?

- When you think about being made in the image or likeness of God, how do you feel?

- When you think about your child, how do these passages inform your thoughts and feelings?

The beauty of the Bible is its ability to continuously impact its reader, no matter the time in history it is read. As modern-day readers, the passage Genesis 1:26–27 should spur us on to modern-day fruitfulness. Some might take that to mean taking care of God's creation. Others might emphasize taking care of the lowest members of society. Later, in the New Testament book of Galatians, the term "fruit" is applied to what those who live by the Spirit do. It states, "By contrast, the fruit of the Spirit is love, joy, peace, patience, kindness, generosity, faithfulness, gentleness, and self-control. There is no law against such things" (Galatians 5:22–23, *NRSV*).

Record your answers to the following questions:

- Which of the fruit of the Spirit (love, joy, peace, patience, kindness, generosity, faithfulness, gentleness, and self-control) does your middle-schooler embody the most?

____

____

____

____

____

- How can you lift up your child's embodiment of (love, joy, peace . . .) to help them embrace them as gifts from God?

____

____

____

____

____

- One of the greatest gifts parents can give their children is to model a healthy understanding of our own bodies. How can you embrace the message in Genesis that you are made in the image of God and you are very good?

The beginning of love is the will to let those we love be perfectly themselves, the resolution not to twist them to fit our own image. If in loving them we do not love what they are, but only their potential likeness to ourselves, then we do not love them: we only love the reflection of ourselves we find in them.[10]

—Thomas Merton

Record your responses to the following:

- Identify some unique qualities that your child embodies that you do not.

10 Merton, Thomas. *No Man Is an Island*. (New York: Harcourt Brace Jovanovich, 1978), 177-178.

- How can you affirm those unique qualities in your child?

Blessing Your Child

Blessing children is a way to express our deepest hopes and dreams for them. Blessing our children is a way to encourage them.

Complete the blessing below. Give that blessing to your child; you can insert it into a lunch bag or slip it under a pillow . . . or just pronounce the blessing at dinner:

> Today you *(insert an action that you observed)*. That reminded me about how God *(describe an action of God)*. You are made in the image of God.
>
> Here is an example:
>
> Today you *stopped to help your little sister when she fell*. That reminded me about how God *cares for us, especially when we are weak and sad*. You are made in the image of God.

SESSION 2

YOU ARE COMPLEX

In today's session, participants explored the concept of sexuality and its complexity. They reflected on Psalm 139 and explored how they are complex and made in the image of God.

Words in the English language fall very short in describing God. The Trinity is often called a *holy mystery* because it does not make sense to the human mind. How is it possible for 1 + 1 + 1 to equal 1? The same mystery is found in humanity. How is it possible to describe such a COMPLEX creation as humanity? Are words like *man* and *woman* enough?

Consider the limitations of using certain words for God. Ask yourself, if I only spoke of God as "Son," what would I miss out on? If I only saw God as "Father," how would I limit my understanding of God? If I only focused on the movement of God as the Holy Spirit, what would I not experience?

In our session we challenged our commonly narrow view of male and female and saw how being just all male or all female was limiting.

Just as God is COMPLEX, so is humanity. After all, we were created in the image of God.

Key Terms

In this session participants differentiated between *biological gender, gender identity, gender expression*, and *attraction*.[11]

Here are some of the terms about sexuality and gender that were introduced to participants:

- *Biological gender* refers to the physical anatomy of an individual's body.
- *Gender identity* is built upon what an individual senses internally.
- *Gender expression* refers to the way a person interprets their gender with outward displays of that gender stereotype.
- *Attraction* refers to when someone is physically drawn to another person or sees someone as desirable.

11 For more information on these terms, readers may find the following resources helpful: Some of this content is the combination of resources including information from a TEDx Talk by Dr. Margaret Nichols, "Beyond the Binary: Understanding Transgender Youth," and these websites:
- http://itspronouncedmetrosexual.com/2012/01/the-genderbread-person/.
- https://www.genderspectrum.org, http://www.glsen.org.
- http://geneq.berkeley.edu/lgbt_resources_definiton_of_terms.

- *Agender* individuals are people who are internally ungendered or do not feel a sense of gender identity.
- *Cisgender* individuals are people who, by nature or by choice, do not conform to gender-based expectations of society.
- *Gender fluid* describes one who moves in and out of different ways of expressing and identifying oneself.
- *Intersex* individuals are born with chromosomes, external genitalia, or internal reproductive systems that do not fall into socially constructed male and female ways of thinking about sex.
- *Pangender* individuals are people whose gender identity is made up of all or many gender expressions.

We Are Known

Psalm 139:13–14 *(New Living Translation):*

> You made all the delicate, inner parts of my body
> and knit me together in my mother's womb.
> Thank you for making me so wonderfully complex!
> Your workmanship is marvelous—how well I know it.

Note the first line of verse 14: "Thank you for making me so wonderfully complex!"

Reflect on the following questions and record your answers in the space provided:

- Thinking back on your life, how did you learn about sexuality?

- What do you want to do differently with your child?

- What values in the area of sexuality do you want to teach your child? What values will your child learn from you? from the church? from friends? from family?

Words of affirmations, love, understanding and acceptance are like the bread and wine of the Eucharist. They nourish, restore, and heal.

Write some messages of love, understanding, and acceptance for your child here. Find ways to deliver those messages through small notes or quiet whispers at night.

A Parenting Prayer

Loving and gracious God, creator and sustainer of all,
Who knows the challenges and joys of adolescence,
Who made us in the image of the God and
calls us "very good,"
Who gives us a ministry that demands our best efforts,
Whose presence fills us with gladness,
We thank you for the community that supports us,
for their generous hearts,
for their abundant gifts,
for their willingness to walk on this journey.
We thank you for giving us this empowering work.
We confess that we may be nervous or anxious.

We acknowledge our tendency to control.
Bless us with calm spirits born of your love.
Bless us with unburdened hearts to listen.
Bless us with patience, humor and joy,
And keep us ever mindful of your love and grace.
Amen.

SESSION 3

YOU ARE ACCEPTED

Creator God, giver of the divine image, hold us tightly within your arms of love so that even when we do not feel beautiful by the standards of the world, we are able to claim your image imprinted on us, in the name of God our life-giver, Jesus our life-redeemer, and Holy Spirit our life-perfecter. Amen.

We know that we are loved and accepted by God, just the way we are, but God believes in us too much to leave us that way.[12] God is working to help us be more Christ-like.

In the New Testament book of Hebrews it states, "In the past, God spoke through the prophets to our ancestors in many

12 Adapted from the statement by Max Lucado, quoted by Presiding Bishop Michael Curry in his sermon at General Convention 2015.

times and many ways. In these final days, though, he spoke to us through a Son. God made his Son the heir of everything and created the world through him. The Son is the light of God's glory and the imprint of God's being. He maintains everything with his powerful message. After he carried out the cleansing of people from their sins, he sat down at the right side of the highest majesty" (Hebrews 1:1–3, *CEB*).

- What does the "imprint of God's being" mean to you in this passage from Hebrews?

Middle-schoolers and adults alike have embedded understandings of human beauty—both internal and external.

Today's kids are bombarded with unrealistic images and are fed a diet of computer-enhanced human images to which they compare their own growing bodies.

According to research from Brown University, body image is a widespread preoccupation. Middle-schoolers, teens, and young adults are preoccupied with their bodies and weight. In the Brown study researchers found that 74% of the normal-weight women and 46% of normal-weight men thought about the way they looked or their weight "all the time" or "frequently."

Letting go of poor body image requires replacing it with an affirmation of our acceptance in the eyes of God.

Reflect on the following questions and record your answers in the space provided:

- What are the images of and ideas about your own body that you want to let go?

- What images of beauty do you want to teach your child?

- What situations or circumstances cause your child to have a distorted view of their body?

Genesis tells us, "God created humanity in God's own image, in the divine image God created them, male and female God created them" (Genesis 1:27). We are each made in the likeness of God. Sometimes, when we have accepted a flawed way of thinking, the first step to correcting it is to hear the truth out loud. Our culture's definition of beauty is flawed, but God's acceptance of us is not built upon that understanding.

We know that God created us and called us good. In Christ, we have an example of the perfect image of God in human form. We also believe that by the power of God at work in our lives through the Holy Spirit, we can gradually look more and more like Christ. This is the journey of a lifetime.

We know that we are loved and accepted by God, just the way we are, but God believes in us too much to leave us that way.[13] God is working to help us be more Christ-like. This is not limited to one aspect of our lives; instead, it is nothing short of a transformation of the body, mind, and spirit.

The New Testament book of Hebrews states, "In the past, God spoke through the prophets to our ancestors in many times and many ways. In these final days, though, he spoke to us through a Son. God made his Son the heir of everything and created the world through him. The Son is the light of God's glory and the imprint of God's being. He maintains everything with his powerful message. After he carried out the cleansing

13 Adapted from the statement by Max Lucado, quoted by Presiding Bishop Michael Curry in his sermon at General Convention 2015.

of people from their sins, he sat down at the right side of the highest majesty" (Hebrews 1:1–3, *CEB*).

In Colossians 1 we read about Jesus. The author states, "The Son is the image of the invisible God, the one who is first over all creation" (Colossians 1:15, *CEB*).

Reflect on the following and record your answers in the space provided:

- What do you think the phrase *imprint of God's being* means in the passage from Hebrews?

- In what ways does your child bear the imprint of God?

- Use this sentence to bless your middle-schooler (and other children, if you have them!): "*(Name)*, you are accepted by God."

SESSION 4

YOU ARE RELATIONAL (PART 1)

O Lord, you have taught us that without love whatever we do is worth nothing: Send your Holy Spirit and pour into our hearts your greatest gift, which is love, the true bond of peace and of all virtue, without which whoever lives is accounted dead before you. Grant this for the sake of your only Son Jesus Christ, who lives and reigns with you and the Holy Spirit, one God, now and forever. Amen.[14]

No one has greater love than this, to lay down one's life for one's friends.
—John 15:13, *NRSV*

14 Seventh Sunday after the Epiphany, Book of Common Prayer, 216.

As children of God, we are relational people—people who are called to love and serve one another. The greatest commandment sets the stage for our intentional mission of loving others. But why are relationships so important in the Christian life? Our relationships are the proving ground of life. Our friendships, our acquaintances, and our intimate, lifelong bonds provide the ground on which we work to become more Christ-like. As relational people we grow up into the full stature of Christ in our relationships—learning to love one another as Christ loved us and to "manifest the grace of God, the gifts of the Spirit, and holiness of life."[15]

Students in middle school have relationships on many different levels. They need examples of friendship and love that is loyal, respectful, mutual, and committed. Reflect on the following and record your answers in the space provided:

- How do love, infatuation, and friendship interplay?

____

____

____

____

____

____

15 Standing Commission of Liturgy and Music, 25.

- What do you want to teach your child about friendship?

Middle-schoolers are exploring the ways in which they can be friends to others and how to nurture the relationships that are most important to them. Reflect on the following and record your response in the space provided:

- Name some ways that your child has been a good friend to others.

Blessing your child is way to instill your values and to name their gifts. Consider completing and sharing these blessings with your middle-schooler:

- When I see you *(identify an action you've observed)*, I can tell you are a good friend.
- When you do or say *(identify an action you've observed)*, I appreciate that you are thinking about and caring for your friends.

SESSION 5

YOU ARE RELATIONAL (PART 2)

Gracious and Loving God,
you have blessed us with the gift of friends and family.
We thank you for the love that enfolds and the freedom to be ourselves.
We thank you for those
who know the love of friendship,
who are patient in listening,
who sit with us when we cry,
who comfort us in pain,
who celebrate with us in joy,
who laugh with us in delight,
who remind us that we are God's children.
Bless our friends with faith, hope, and love.
Amen.

Middle-schoolers look for ways to build relationships and to practice relationship skills. Encouraging them to clarify their thoughts and feelings about friendships and family relationships helps them strengthen interpersonal skills.

Thinking about your own relationships, complete these sentences in the space provided:

- Friendship is . . .

- True friendship feels like . . .

- Being a friend means . . .

- Friendships are sometimes hard when . . .

- A friend will *(use verbs—action words)* . . .

The definition of *love* is not simple. The scriptures record the relationship between David and Jonathan (explored in Session 4) as one that is complex. The same for the relationship between Ruth and Naomi (explored in Session 5). So it is with most of the relationships in the Bible—and in real life!

Reflect on the following and record your answers in the space provided:

- What are some other relationships or stories in the Bible that are complex?

- What you do want to teach your child about relationships and their complexity?

SESSION 6

YOU ARE RESPONSIBLE

Therefore, as a prisoner for the Lord, I encourage you to live as people worthy of the call you received from God. Conduct yourselves with all humility, gentleness, and patience. Accept each other with love, and make an effort to preserve the unity of the Spirit with the peace that ties you together.

—Ephesians 4:1–3, *NRSV*

Fire provides a good analogy for sexuality, providing a way to talk about both *promise* and *risk*. The "use" of sexuality (like the use of fire) calls for maturity and safe practice, while always recognizing its inherent beauty as a gift from God.

Reflect on these affirmations about sex:

- Sexuality is a *gift* from God.
- Sexuality is a gift born of *love* and to be used with love, never as manipulation or violence, nor casually.
- Using your sexuality when you are not mature enough is full of *risk* and can be *dangerous*.

In the space provided, record your answers to the following questions:

- What are the promises of sexual intercourse—where is the beauty?

- How can you model and teach your child that their bodies and sexuality are a gift from God?

- How can you help your middle-schooler discern what protections (guidelines and rules) they need as they mature and enter into more mature relationships?

- What milestones come to mind and what would you want to teach at those milestones? *Example: Going to a movie without a parent. Teach them to stay with friends and to stick with the plan.*

- Middle-schoolers are looking for love, affection, and acceptance. How can this model of a mature love help you define an ideal love for your child?

SESSION 7

YOU ARE KNOWLEDGEABLE

In Session 7, participants played a Fact or Fiction game to learn more about the complexities of sexuality and to practice discernment.

In the following chart, you'll find the answers to the Fact or Fiction game played in the session. Participants were asked to identify whether the statements in the first column were "Fact" or "Fiction." You'll find commentary in the third column.

1. Most teenagers have had sexual intercourse.	FICTION	While it is true that about half of all teenagers (15–19 years old) have had sexual intercourse, it is also true that about half have *not* had intercourse.

Percentage of never-married teenagers 15–19 years of age who have ever had intercourse, by age and sex: United States, 2002, 2006–2010 and 2011–2013

Female	2002	2006–2010	2011–2013
15–19 years of age	45.5%	42.6%	44.1%
15–17 years of age	30.3%	27.0%	30.2%
18–19 years of age	68.8%	62.7%	64.4%

Male	2002	2006–2010	2011–2013
15–19 years of age	45.7%	41.8%	46.8%
15–17 years of age	31.3%	28.0%	34.4%
18–19 years of age	64.3%	63.9%	64.0%

Sources:

Vital and Health Statistics, Teenagers in the United States: Sexual Activity, Contraceptive Use, and Childbearing, 2006–2010 National Survey of Family Growth Series 23, Number 31 October 2011

NCHS Data Brief, No. 209, July 2015 U.S. DEPARTMENT OF HEALTH AND HUMAN SERVICES Centers for Disease Control and Prevention National Center for Health Statistics Sexual Activity, Contraceptive Use, and Childbearing of Teenagers Aged 15–19 in the United States, Gladys M. Martinez, Ph.D.; and Joyce C. Abma, Ph.D.

2. Once a person who is biologically female has her first period, she can become pregnant.	FACT	When a biologically female person starts having her menstrual period, it means that her reproductive organs have begun working and that she can become pregnant. It does not mean, however, that the body is ready to have a baby. Teen mothers often deliver premature babies. To be ready to have a child involves many aspects, including readiness cognitively, psychologically, spiritually, emotionally, relationally, and economically.
3. For a biologically female person to bathe or swim during her period is unhealthy.	FICTION	There is no reason for women to restrict any activity during their period.
4. The sperm cell from the male determines the biological sex of a baby.	FACT	The sperm cell provides the genetic message that determines gender.
5. A teenager does not need parental consent to get birth control from a clinic.	FACT & FICTION	Family planning clinics in most states don't have to tell anyone (parents included) in order to provide birth control to teenagers. However, in some states parents do have to give their consent in order for teenagers to get birth control.

6. Sexually transmitted infections (STIs) occur without having any symptoms.	FACT	While some STIs have quite recognizable symptoms, others may not. Gonorrhea and chlamydia, for example, display no symptoms in females and often are undetectable in males. A doctor's examination is important if a person thinks they may have an STI.
7. If a biologically female person is not menstruating by the time she is 16, there is something wrong.	FICTION	Absolutely not. For a biologically female individual to begin having a period as early as age 8 or as late as 16 or 17 is perfectly normal. If a female is 16 and is worried because she has not yet started menstruating, she can always see a doctor to ensure everything is okay.
8. A biologically female person can get pregnant from sex during her period.	FACT	A biologically female person can get pregnant any time during her menstrual cycle, including during her period.
9. Birth control pills cause cancer.	FICTION	Though side effects can occur from using the pill, there is no conclusive evidence that the pill causes cancer.
10. Only LGBTQ+ (lesbian, gay, bisexual, transgender, queer) people and drug users are at risk for HIV AIDS.	FICTION	While sex between two men and intravenous drug use remain the largest exposure categories, people infected through heterosexual contact comprise the fastest-growing segment of the AIDS population.

11. In order for sperm to be manufactured, the temperature in the testicles must be slightly cooler than normal body temperature, but not too cool.	FACT	Sperm cells can only be manufactured in the testicles when they are slightly cooler than body temperature. The scrota acts like a temperature gauge. When a biologically male body is warm the testicles are allowed to hang away from the body. When it is cold (cold air or cold water), the scrotum draws the testicles up closer to the body to keep them from being too cool.
12. Teenagers can be treated for sexually transmitted infections without their parent's permission.	Depends	Laws vary, but most states require parental permission to provide treatment for STIs to teenagers.
13. Alcohol and marijuana are sexual stimulants.	FICTION	There really are no sexual stimulants. Alcohol and marijuana lessen an individual's inhibitions but they do not stimulate sexual activity.
14. There is one absolutely safe time between menstrual cycles when a biologically female individual cannot get pregnant.	FICTION	Because of the variability of the menstrual and ovulation cycle, the time when the egg is present cannot be determined exactly.

15. Wet dreams happen to every biologically male individual.	FICTION	Some people do not have nocturnal emissions.
16. When a rape occurs, the rapist is usually a stranger.	FICTION	The majority of rapes are perpetrated by someone known to the victim.
17. Once an erection occurs and an individual is excited, without intercourse there can be physical harm.	FICTION	An erection is not actually painful. Erections have occurred since an individual was a fetus. An erection will go away on its own.
18. A female can get pregnant even if a male does not ejaculate or "come" inside of her.	FACT	A woman can get pregnant even if her partner "comes" outside of her body. During foreplay, oral sex, or intercourse, semen, which contains sperm, seeps out of the penis.
19. If a female misses her period, she is definitely pregnant.	FICTION	There are many reasons a person might miss a period. Some medications and even exercise can suppress a person's menstrual cycle.

20. You cannot get HIV/AIDS from touching things that a person with HIV/AIDS has used.	FACT	HIV/AIDS is not transmitted by casual contact like sharing drinks, or cups, hugging, kissing, or holding hands.
21. Virginity can be proven.	FICTION	You cannot tell people's sexual histories by looking at them or by engaging in sexual activity, including sexual intercourse.
22. Females who start having sexual intercourse before the age of 16 are more likely to get pregnant than those who wait until they are over 18 to have sex.	FACT	People who have sex before they are 16 have a higher rate of pregnancy due to the lack of birth control. Many teenagers are not prepared for sexual intercourse and do not engage in "safer sex."
23. Biologically female individuals are born with all of their eggs in their ovaries.	FACT	The eggs inside a female's ovaries are developed when she is a fetus inside her mother's uterus. Women do not produce more eggs over their lifetime. Although the eggs are in the ovaries as a baby and child, they are undeveloped.
24. Oral sex is safe because you cannot get pregnant or contract STIs.	FICTION	STIs are transmitted by the touching of genital areas or mouths. Oral sex doesn't protect from STIs. An individual can get pregnant even if the partner "comes" outside of her body. During foreplay, oral sex or intercourse, semen, which contains sperm, seeps out of the penis.

25. There is nothing wrong with looking at pornography.	FICTION	Pornography is sexually explicit images. Those images are a distortion of God's creation. People in pornography are seen as objects of sexual pleasure and not as children of God. We should strive to behave in such a way that shows respect for all people. Pornography is also addictive; looking at pornography leads people to want to look at more and more sexually explicit material.
26. Drinking alcohol leads to the same effects for adults and teenagers.	FACT & FICTION	Alcohol is a drug, a legal drug for those 21 and older. Although drinking alcohol is legal for adults and not for teenagers, there are other reasons to avoid alcohol use as a teenager. Because teens are still growing and maturing, the risks and dangers associated with alcohol use are greater for teens than for adults. Drinking alcohol negatively affects an adolescent's growing body and brain. Because teenagers' brains are not fully developed, their impulse control and willingness to delay gratification are not fully developed, which can lead to poor decision-making. In both adults and teens, alcohol hinders decision-making skills and loosens natural inhibitions leading to risky behaviors.
27. Consuming alcohol does not affect decision-making.	FICTION	In both adults and teens, alcohol hinders decision-making skills.

28. Inaccurate as well as accurate information about sexuality can be found on the Internet.	FACT	The Internet can be a good resource for information and it can also provide false or incomplete information. As with any source of information, remember to "consider the source" before you believe something that you read or hear.
29. Masturbation is a normal part of a person's sexuality.	FACT	Although our society used to think that masturbation was "bad," we now know that masturbation is a normal part of sexuality.
30. Drugs and alcohol do not have anything to do with sexual activity.	FICTION	The decision to engage in activity or sexual intercourse is based on judgment. Both alcohol and drugs impair judgment and loosen natural inhibitions. A person who is using alcohol or drugs may find that they do something that they normally wouldn't do, like engage in sexual activity.

After reviewing the information in the chart, take some time to record your responses to the following:

- Identify three bits of information found in the chart that you already knew.

____

____

____

____

____

- Identify three things you learned.

- Identify three things you would like to explore further.

- From the chart, what areas would you like to discuss with your middle-schooler? (Once you've listed these, plan on tackling them one at a time!)

SESSION 8

YOU ARE CONNECTED

Holy God, one who took on flesh and lived as one of us,
dwell with us here and give us courage to learn, grow,
and become more like you,
that we may be more loving, kind, and full of grace,
through God our Creator, Christ our Redeemer, and
the Spirit our Sustainer. Amen.

INTERVIEW GUIDE

As you interview your daughter or son, invite them to describe how their *faith*, *community*, and *family values* influence the answers they give.

- What have you heard about dating?
- Do kids your age date?
- What do you think about that?
- What are some of the things you have seen in movies, on TV, on the Internet, or on the radio about sex?
- Do any of the things you have heard bother you?
- Do you feel like you can come to me with your questions about sexuality and sex?
- Are you comfortable with your development? Does anything worry you?
- When you think about your gender, how do you best describe yourself?
- What are three things you look for in a person to whom you are attracted?
- Is there anything you would like to share with me?

Reflect on the experience of interviewing another person. In some ways, I wonder if the interviews you conducted could be compared to a story in the Old Testament.

It is a story of a conversation with God. This story reminds us that a conversation is supposed to include speaking and listening.

In the story of Elijah in 1 Kings 19, Elijah has a conversation with God. The Bible tells us that Elijah had spent the night in a cave and was truly at the end of his rope. The conversation he had with God is beautiful because it includes both speaking and listening.

The word of the Lord told Elijah to go outside of the cave and wait for the LORD to pass by (1Kings 19:11). At first, there was a great wind that split the mountains and broke rocks into pieces (1 Kings 19:11). Then there was an earthquake and then a fire (1 Kings 19:12). In the story we are told that the LORD was not in the wind, the fire, or the earthquake. Finally, the passage says, "And after the fire a sound of sheer silence" (1 Kings 19:12).

It was in the silence that Elijah came out of the cave and spoke with God.

If you were going to describe your interview today, would you call it a *great wind*? How about an earthquake? Perhaps *fire*? I invite you to describe your interview as one of these three pictures: *wind, fire*, or *earthquake*. For example, you might say, "My interview was like a *fire* because . . ."

FIVE TO DECIDE

In today's session, titled *You Are CONNECTED*, you played the Five to Decide game. You made choices about statements, deciding whether you agreed or disagreed.

Soon after the session, reflect for a few minutes on the activity, writing your answers to the following questions:

- What did you learn about your child?

- What did you learn about yourself?

- What questions surprised you the most?

SESSION 9

YOU ARE EMPOWERED

i longed to lift the burden of your sorrow and yet,
i knew it was yours to carry.
and so i walked next to you. side by side.
i rested when you rested.
cried when you cried.
and loved you more with each step of the road.[16]

16 Used with permission of terri st. cloud, bone sigh arts www.BoneSighArts.com.

> [1]If then there is any encouragement in Christ, any consolation from love, any sharing in the Spirit, any compassion and sympathy, [2]make my joy complete: be of the same mind, having the same love, being in full accord and of one mind. [3]Do nothing from selfish ambition or conceit, but in humility regard others as better than yourselves. [4]Let each of you look not to your own interests, but to the interests of others. [5]Let the same mind be in you that was in Christ Jesus . . .
>
> —Philippians 2:2–5, *NRSV*

In today's session, participants explored the empowering value of *assertiveness*.

Part of being responsible is using positive skills to express your values. Assertiveness is one of those skills that will help your middle-schooler make good decisions and stand up for what they value.

Assertiveness is a *positive* way of standing up for yourself (as opposed to aggression). Assertive behavior includes communicating what is important to you or what you feel in a firm way that does not insult or attack the other person. When you are assertive, you state your own thoughts and feelings and take ownership of them. You don't blame others for your feelings. You tell people how their behavior affects you.

Assertive communication is effective because it is honest, open, and nonaggressive. You will feel good about how you communicate when you are assertive. Things may not always go your way, and people may not agree with you, but you will be standing up for yourself in a kind and loving way.

Reflect on the following questions and record your answers in the space provided:

- What are some situations that you can remember needing to be assertive?

- Did you struggle with assertiveness? or with being aggressive?

- What are the most important aspects of assertiveness to you?

- How can you empower your child to be more assertive and less aggressive?

SESSION 10

YOU ARE THOUGHTFUL

Do not be conformed to this world, but be transformed by the renewing of your minds, so that you may discern what is the will of God—what is good and acceptable and perfect.

—Romans 12:2

O heavenly Father, who hast filled the world with beauty: Open our eyes to behold thy gracious hand in all thy works; that, rejoicing in thy whole creation, we may learn to serve thee with gladness; for the sake of him through whom all things were made, thy Son Jesus Christ our Lord.[17]

17 Book of Common Prayer, For Joy in God's Creation, 814.

Giving young people the opportunity to explore their values in the light of the gospel of grace and love enables them to "own" those values. When they leave the protection of church or home, their values will inform their decisions and empower them to take actions that align with those values.

Today's session assured participants: *Our God and our families care because they love you. God loves you unconditionally. God wants what is best in your life and what will make you most fulfilled.*

Reflect on the following questions and record your answers in the space provided:

- What are your dreams and hopes for your child?

- How will you empower you middle-schooler as they grow and mature?

- When the rough times come and you are feeling lost, where can you turn for support and encouragement?

- How can the church help you in raising this precious child?

Grant to us, Lord, we pray, the spirit to think and do always those things that are right, that we, who cannot exist without you, may by you be enabled to live according to your will; through Jesus Christ our Lord, who lives and reigns with you and the Holy Spirit, one God, for ever and ever.[18] *Amen.*

18 Book of Common Prayer, 232.

Consider using this blessing with your family:

Parent: The Lord bless you and keep you.
Family: Amen.
Parent: The Lord make his face to shine upon you and be gracious to you.
Family: Amen.
Parent: The Lord lift up his countenance upon you and give you peace.
Family: Amen.

RESOURCES

Authors' note to parents:

These Are Our Bodies (Foundation Book) has an extensive glossary, bibliography, and overview of adolescent development that we recommend for your own information as well as to support and understand your child. Your child's *Participant Book* includes additional anatomical and physiological terms; you may find it helpful to review this with your child in order to better understand the terms they are learning.

Organizations

- **The Center for Lesbian & Gay Studies in Religion and Ministry**: Has a mission to advance the well-being of lesbian, gay, bisexual, queer, and transgender people and to transform faith communities and the wider society by taking a leading role in shaping a new public discourse on religion, gender identity, and sexuality through education, research, community building, and advocacy. http://clgs.org.

- **The Coalition for Positive Sexuality**: Offers information in English and Spanish for young people who are sexually active or considering sexual activity. http://positive.org.
- **Common Sense Media**: A trusted media education resource offers questions and answers regarding privacy and the Internet. www.commonsensemedia.org/privacy-and-internet-safety.
- **Faith Trust Institute**: A national, multifaith, multicultural, training and education organization that works to end sexual and domestic violence. www.faithtrustinstitute.org.
- **Integrity USA**: An organization "proclaiming God's inclusive love in and through the Episcopal Church since 1975. www.integrityusa.org.
- **Religious Institute**: A multifaith organization dedicated to advocating for sexual health, education, and just in faith communities and societies. www.religiousinstitute.org.
- **Stop Bullying**: Information, videos, lessons, and more to respond to bullying. www.stopbullying.gov.
- **Trans Student Educational Resources**: A youth-led organization dedicated to transforming the educational environment for trans and gender non-conforming students through advocacy and empowerment. In addition to creating a more trans-friendly education system, their mission is to

educate the public and teach trans activists how to be effective organizers. TSER believes that justice for trans and gender non-conforming youth is contingent on an intersectional framework of activism. Ending oppression is a long-term process that can only be achieved through collaborative action. www.transstudent.org.

Print and Online Resources

- Berman, Laura. *Talking to Your Kids About Sex: Turning "The Talk" into a Conversation for Life*. New York: DK Publishing, 2009.
- Brill, Stephanie and Pepper, Rachel. *The Transgender Child: A Handbook for Families and Professionals*. San Francisco, CA: Cleis Press, Inc., 2008.
- Dykstra, Robert C., Allan Hugh Cole Jr., and Donald Capps. *Losers, Loners, and Rebels: The Spiritual Struggles of Boys*. Louisville: Westminster John Knox Press, 2007.
- _____. *The Faith and Friendship of Teenage Boys*. Louisville: Westminster John Knox Press, 2012.
- Gomes, Peter J. *The Good Book: Reading the Bible with Mind and Heart*. San Francisco: HarperSanFrancisco, 1996.
- Harris, Robie. *It's Not the Stork! A Book About Girls, Boys, Babies, Bodies, Families and Friends*. Somerville, MA: Candlewick Press, 2008.

- _____. *It's So Amazing! A Book about Eggs, Sperm, Birth, Babies, and Families.* Somerville, MA: Candlewick Press, 2014.
- _____. *It's Perfectly Normal: Changing Bodies, Growing Up, Sex, and Sexual Health*. Somerville: MA, Candlewick Press, 2014.
- Mercer, Joyce Ann. *GirlTalk/GodTalk: Why Faith Matters to Teenage Girls and Their Parents*. San Francisco: Jossey-Bass, 2008.
- Nelson, James B. *Embodiment: An Approach to Sexuality and Christian Theology*. Minneapolis: Augsburg Publications, 1978.
- Smith, Christian and Melinda Lundquist Denton. *Soul Searching: The Religious and Spiritual Lives of American Teenagers*. New York: Oxford University Press, 2005.
- Smith, Christian and Patricia Snell. *Souls in Transition: The Religious and Spiritual Lives of Emerging Adults*. New York: Oxford University Press, 2009.
- Tigert, Leanne McCall and Timothy Brown, eds. *Coming Out Young and Faithful*. Cleveland: Pilgrim Press, 2001.
- Valenti, Jessica. *The Purity Myth: How America's Obsession with Virginity Is Hurting Young Women*. Berkeley, CA: Seal Press, 2010.